Search Me!

Circāre: The Art Of The Question

Dr. Peter Q John (JD, MBA)

"This book eliminates uncomfortable small talk in everyday situations while letting you know what people really think."

–**Danielle Glass**, *CPO, Chica de partido de professional, Owner of Thepartygirlguide.com,* 从地球

Aspect Books

PRINTED IN
THE UNITED STATES OF AMERICA

Model appearance in this book does not mean they are involved with the author! Follow the Search Me! contract. Please consult a licensed counselor or therapist if this book exposes communication difficulties in your relationship

---

Cover design by Vivian Vu

ISBN-13: 978-1-57258-653-6 (Paperback)
ISBN-13: 978-1-57258-654-3 (eBook)
Library of Congress Control Number: 2010919537

Published by
Aspect Books

Dedication

Get to know your friends and loved ones better

Acknowledgements

Special thanks to my friends the beautiful young talented models: Amp, Danielle, Elijah, Lorenzo, PLUS, King, Vivian. Credit and thanks to photographers; LookBook LA, Tom Huynh, Los Angeles, Keith Majors Photography NY. IPad and other readers e-book available, request it from your local book store or online. For public speaking bookings; www.talkcalm.com For questions, suggestions for the next ***Search Me!*** chapter, or comments about this book, your feedback is welcomed cirjon@yahoo.com.

Table of Contents

Introduction

Experience the magic

Read this first chapter of this book. Accept the simple structure. The first three chapters will teach you how to talk by teaching you how to listen respectfully.

Chapter 1:

The Matrix of Respect

The matrix of this book is a direct approach that facilitates practical social interaction. Day-to-day people engage in too much cowardly quick electronic communication such as text where anything can be sent without the responsibility and respect of a direct question or a direct reaction. Our overall quality of direct communication is diminishing. This book is based on a principle of self authenticity and respect. Use it to talk. **Search Me!** is designed to replace vague everyday e-talk and replaces it with authentic information.

Individual inherent value is recognized by the neutral tone of the questions. Your innate personal value, beauty and ideas make **Search Me!** a uniquely magical book.

The natural limits of life will be warmly shared and become evident to you and your talk-pal. A natural comfortable connection between all people will also become evident increasing the richness of the "share-talk" experience.

Search Me! is designed to function as a manual-analogue-search engine of the highest order driven by a neurological processor functioning on a platform unable to be duplicated by any existing commercial search engine. Consider **Search Me**! as a tool, like the original Google or Yahoo that you have full control of; you own it. The only limit of this search engine is life and imagination. Use life, love and harmony as your guides in this style of direct social interaction. Much of communication is non-verbal. With so much communication happening electronically, **Search Me!** is a step backwards away from tweet, text and small talk to real talk.

This search engine works best when you just accept the other person's response(s), move on, and ask another question.

When you are finished using this book, smile and say thank you, bow, and hug or shake hands. Whatever works for you. Touch the other person because you did already by letting yourself be searched and by you searching someone else. Something magical happens when we interact directly and honestly. Search me and you will feel it.

Chapter 2:

How It Works

This book works best with a few controls (rules). There must be at least two people to share this book or it makes no sense at all. This book comes alive like volleyball or tennis when two or more people are taking turns sharing together. The more people involved, the merrier the group. Group size will affect time consumption.

Search Me! is a dinner book. Invite someone to dinner or on a first date, and hours will easily pass as you search one another.

Let the other person choose the topic first and you ask the questions. The person asking the question cannot

answer or comment on the answer given. An answer just has to be accepted. ***Serve the questions and keep it moving*!**

Take turns asking questions when topics change. One person asks all questions to the other person or group on a particular topic; i.e., one narrator for each topic.

The pace should be like a volley ball game with questions being tossed back and forth. Do not get bogged down in one area. Serve a question and *Keep it moving!*

There is no explaining. A response to a question is information and that is all. Only the person answering the question can decide if they want to explain the response given. It is very important that a question is not answered with a question or dead-end ambiguity. For example if the person answering says, it depends, on what you are asking…, that is ambiguous. The person answering should analyze the potential options and choose and commit to a response.

If a person insists on answering a question with a question, he or she must provide an answer to his or her own question and fill in conditional responses with facts or scenarios that will provide a more informative response. Conditional responses/answers must be elaborated!

Laughing is greatly encouraged. Smiling while asking questions is greatly encouraged and is likely difficult to avoid doing because searching someone sparks fun. When you read and share this book together, respect and acknowledge openness and creativity. Do not judge. Be open minded. There is no right or wrong answer(s).

Just be OPEN

This is not a court room examination. It is simple "share-talk", sharing life information in a fun comfortable way. Significant differences in answers and responses to simple questions are to be expected and embraced. Similarities in answers are also to be expected. That is the beauty of the search.

A fun book to help you laugh at life

Chapter 3:

How To Keep It Light And Fun

Eye contact, light and fun…

Words and statements such as you are wrong, that's not true, that's weird, etc..., are strictly prohibited. Only words such as interesting, wow, and okay can be used as a response to the person who answered a question. You can ask someone to elaborate or explain, but you can only respond to that explanation or elaboration with words such as *interesting, wow*, or *okay*.

The Touch Of Talk

Eye contact should be high. Make as much eye contact as you can handle. There is no point made in this book. There are no politics. There is no point advocated by the structure or form of the questions in this book. No one is accepting or advocating anything in this book. This book is not a personality or morality test. **Search Me!** is not an intelligence test. This book is not a test! It works best with food or drinks. Keep your conclusions to yourself and put away your stereotypes and just search me! Enjoy listening to the spontaneous stories that are sparked by this talk tool.

We should not feel threatened by others or uncomfortable with our true feelings and ideas about issues in life. Although similar in many ways, humans reasoning and thinking vary based on individual perception of events. Environment and events shape our thoughts. We all have a hardwired desire to be different. Each person has a unique thinking code. Our processing of issues and opinion are therefore respectfully different. **Search Me!**

Search Me! Contract

(everybody read or repeats)

1. I hereby agree to treat this experience as a fun exchange of honesty and not as an argument.
2. I will not become angry, upset, or argumentative.
3. I will not use the information I learn as the basis for a later argument or action.
4. I will not use judgmental words or statements.
5. I will not make any negative comments or any type of negative communication in response to any answer or response given while using this book.

Chapter 4:

The Search Begins

I swear its true

Lying

1. What is a lie
2. Is lying necessary
3. Why do we lie
4. Does everyone lie
5. Is there such a thing as a small lie
6. If a young child asks, "Where do babies come from?", what should be the response
7. If someone asks a person for his or her name and number, is it ok to give a fake name and wrong number
8. Do lies make us feel better
9. Who do we lie to most
10. Should we lie about serious illnesses
11. Should we lie and tell a young child that daddy has gone away if you know dad just got killed
12. Is it ever necessary to live a lie
13. Should we lie about why we cannot go to work

14. Do married people sometimes live a lie
15. Is Heaven a lie
16. Is fear a part of lying
17. Is it bad to live a lie
18. Is a boob job a lie
19. If a person cheats and gets away with it, should he or she leave this undisclosed and just stop cheating
20. If a very happy person has one day left to live but does not know, should he or she be told
21. Does our government lie
22. Do parents lie
23. Will the truth set a person free

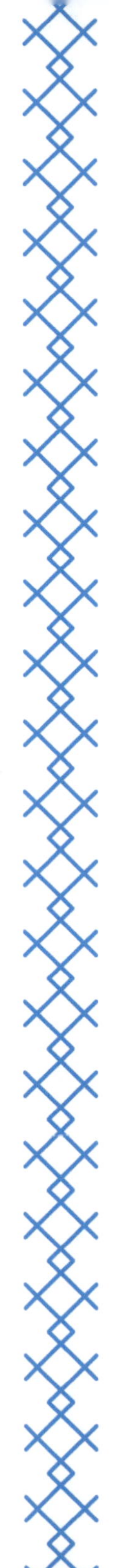

Love or lust

Love

1. Who can love
2. Who cannot love
3. Is love a want
4. Can a person create or make love
5. Is love good
6. Is love bad
7. Do all people deserve love
8. Does love have to be shown to be real
9. Can love be bought
10. Can love be sold
11. Is sex connected to love
12. Is love more a 1-way or 2-way street

13. Should love be earned or given freely
14. Is having sex "making" love
15. Should love be expected
16. Can love change
17. Is love an emotion
18. Is love a feeling
19. Is love actions
20. Should love stay the same
21. Can real love happen at first sight
22. What is love enough for…
23. Is loving too much a bad thing
24. Can love hurt
25. Why does love hurt
26. Can a dead person be loved
27. Is love the same as care
28. Should people be kind to the people they love all the time
29. Are hate and love connected

30. Does loving have rules
31. Who makes the rules of love
32. What happens if the rules of love are broken
33. Does love dictate behavior
34. Do people hide love
35. Is it love if it is hidden
36. Can people fall out of love
37. Is getting care and kindness better than getting just love
38. Is respect related to love
39. Is sacrifice sometimes necessary for love to exist
40. Does everyone want love
41. Why is love blind
42. Is it possible to love 2 people romantically at the same time
43. Is it possible to love someone and hate them at the same time

I really need a moment to think about it

Thoughts

1. What is a thought
2. Where do thoughts come from
3. When does thought occur
4. Why do thoughts happen
5. Are we connected to our thoughts
6. Do we always think
7. What is conscience
8. What is consciousness
9. How are thoughts related to conscience
10. What is a belief
11. Are thoughts random
12. What is an idea
13. Are ideas thoughts
14. Are ideas random

15. Is conscience inward or outward

16. What is good

17. What is evil

18. What is choice

19. Are choice and thoughts connected

20. Do we always think before we act

21. Can we read thoughts of other people

22. Do other people expect us to read their thoughts sometimes

23. How are thoughts connected to feelings

24. Can we stop thinking

25. Can thoughts be manipulated

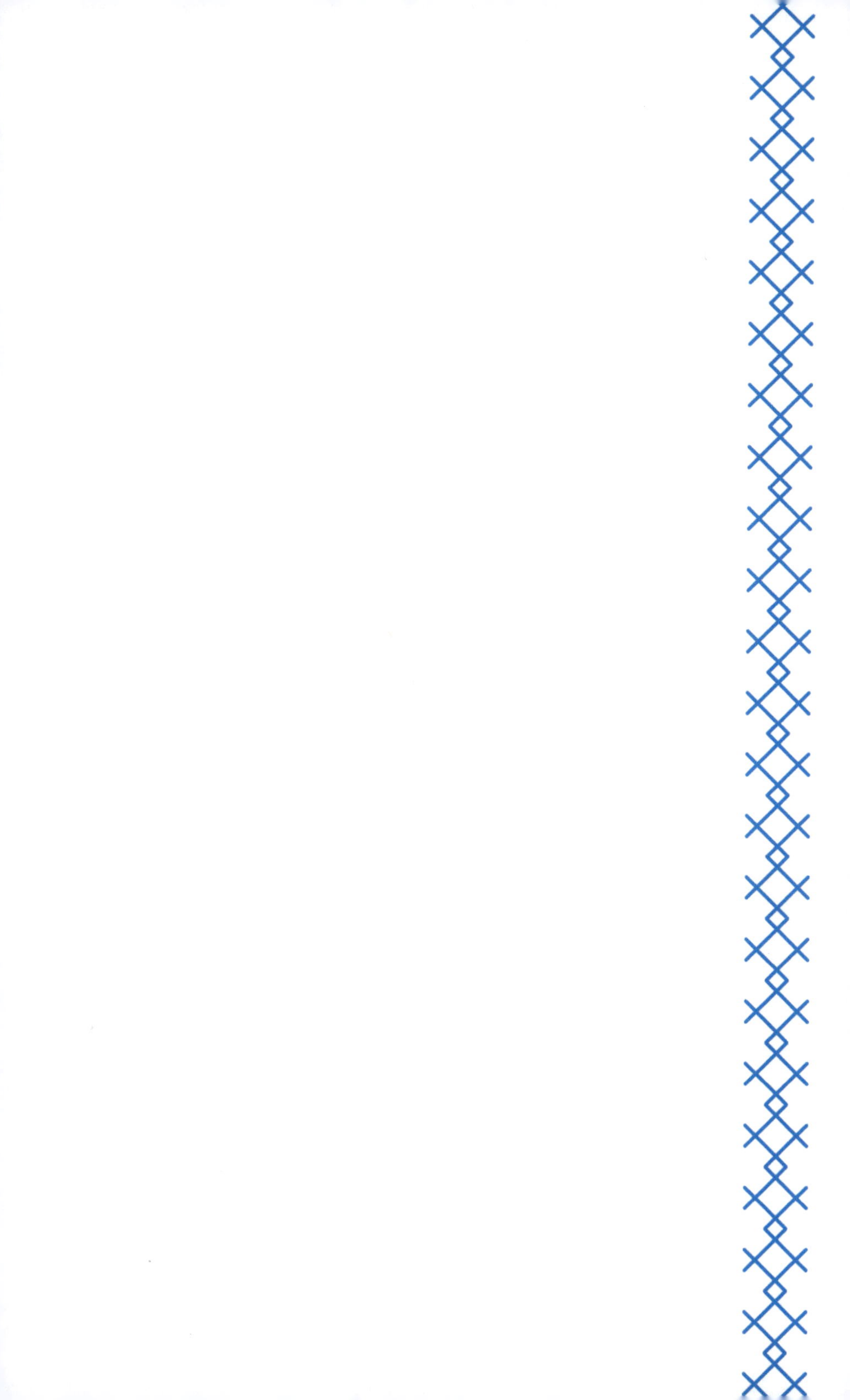

How can we make this work

Relationship

1. What is a relationship
2. How does one get started
3. How does it end
4. Why does it end
5. Do relationships have to end happily
6. Can we have a relationship with anyone
7. How do relationships change
8. Do relationships have rules
9. Who makes the rules for a relationship
10. What happens when the rules are broken
11. Should relationships have names
12. Should relationships have written contracts
13. Do agreements help relationships
14. Are relationships a want or a need

15. Do relationships need boundaries or can they be open
16. What is an open relationship
17. Are relationships necessary for sex
18. Are children better off in a two parent relationship
19. Is trust part of a relationship
20. How does history affect a relationship
21. Can getting married hurt a good relationship
22. When should a relationship be based on need
23. Should a relationship have secrets
24. What kinds of secrets should not be disclosed in a relationship
25. What kind of information should always be disclosed in a relationship
26. How does a best friend differ from a sister or brother
27. Should we be able to terminate marriages by agreement without going to court
28. Why do we mess up good relationships
29. Is giving nothing better than giving the wrong thing

in a relationship

30. Is taking what is freely given dishonest when what is needed is different

31. Do people stay in relationships just to use other people when they really do not like them

32. Should current boyfriend or girlfriend be jealous of previous boyfriend or girlfriend

33. When should former boyfriends or girlfriend get together

34. Why Should couples share email and other internet based account passwords and access

35. When should someone break up with a jealous partner

Blind faith

Faith

1. What is faith
2. Where does faith come from
3. Is it a need
4. Is faith an excuse
5. Is faith a belief
6. Do all people have faith
7. Do dogs have faith
8. Is faith rational
9. Can faith be irrational
10. Can faith be bought
11. Can faith be sold
12. Is faith good
13. Is faith bad
14. Do children have faith

15. Is faith related to spirituality
16. Is faith related to religion
17. Are religion and faith the same
18. Can faith be taught
19. Does faith have to be accepted to exist
20. Is the rejection of faith bad
21. What is spirituality
22. What is religion
23. Is religion an act of faith
24. Is faith more a thought or action
25. Should we expect others to accept our faith
26. Is faith related to peace
27. Is faith related to hate
28. Do we need faith to be happy
29. What is doubt
30. Is doubt better than faith
31. Can faith change fate
32. Is it wrong to doubt

?????????????????

Ok, I'm done talking

Communication

1. Why do we communicate
2. What is communication
3. What is the simplest way to communicate
4. What is the most effective way to communicate
5. What is the worst way to communicate
6. What is the best way to communicate
7. When should we communicate
8. How should we communicate
9. When should people not communicate
10. What is bad communication
11. How does good communication feel
12. What should never be communicated
13. What should always be communicated
14. Who should never be communicated with

15. Who should always be communicated with
16. Are there things that must be communicated in person
17. When are things better communicated electronically (text, phone, etc.)
18. What things are better communicated in person
19. How does volume affect communication
20. Does volume make communication more effective
21. Do places affect communication
22. Does education affect good communication
23. Does lack of education cause poor communication
24. Does emotion affect communication
25. Does humor hurt or help communication
26. When does humor hurt communication
27. Is listening a part of communication
28. Is hearing different from listening
29. Who makes the rules for communication
30. Do schools teach children communication
31. Who or what affects a child's communication the

most: school, friends, or parents?

32. Do relationships fail because of communication
33. Is communication a skill
34. What is the biggest part of communication
35. Why do we use spoken words to communicate
36. Are words or body language important in communication
37. What should we never say
38. What should we never ask
39. When should people who don't communicate well separate

Doctor, Professor, or Lawyer?

Work

1. Is a doctor more valuable than a football player
2. Should we give special treatment to women who are at work
3. Why do we get paid to work
4. Why do we get paid for training
5. Should CEOs get paid for training
6. Why do some people hate their jobs
7. Do stay at home moms deserve a pay check from the federal or state government
8. At what age should children (minors) be allowed to work legally
9. What age should children (minors) be allowed to start a business
10. Do teachers get paid fairly for their work
11. Where does work ethic come from

12. What jobs are too much work for the pay
13. Do children limit one's ability to work
14. Should a preacher get paid
15. What is a bad job
16. What is a good job
17. Should bosses & managers be evaluated for temperament
18. Should teenagers go to work before their first year of college
19. Should all high school students be required to have a job
20. Should undocumented aliens be allowed to work in the US for less money
21. Should older people get the same pay as young people
22. Should mothers get paid the same as single people
23. Should married people be allowed to work together at the same jobs
24. Should married men who have affairs with someone they work with be fired

25. Should married women who have affairs with someone they work with be fired

26. Should people wear very tight fitted clothes to work

27. Should people who are bad at their job be reported

28. Should people who have conflicts at work be required to talk about it before being reported to management

29. Should people on salary get paid when they make mistakes at work

30. Should telecommuting be used to eliminate driving to work

31. Should teachers have to pay to go to college

32. Should people be allowed to have sex at work

33. Should people be allowed to take time off whenever they want to – with pay

We control your mind...you are smiling now

Children

1. Should women be required to get a license to get pregnant
2. Should fathers be prepared to pay child support if they give up parental rights
3. Should parents ever be allowed to spank their children
4. How many children is a reasonable amount for a single person to have
5. How many children should a family have
6. Should children be allowed to have their own phones
7. Should children be allowed to change their names in high school
8. Should children be given the right to make their own choices
9. Which child should be the 1st: a boy or girl

10. Should children be allowed to switch parents if they do not like their parents
11. Should parents clean a child's room
12. When should children have chores
13. When should children be allowed to have a private conversation
14. What age should children be taught about sex
15. At what age should children be before they can choose if they want to go to church
16. When should children be allowed to play
17. When should children be allowed to skip school
18. When should children be given away
19. When should children be yelled at
20. When should children be punished
21. When should children be given money
22. Should parents spoil a child
23. Should a child's opinion count in parental decisions
24. What age should a child's opinion not count in parents decisions

25. Should children have to live with parents who are never home

26. Should parents give children a mandatory minimum amount of time daily

27. Should children be told the truth at all times

Promise, I will pay you back…one day

Money

1. Do money problems and other problems in general come together
2. Why is nothing in life really free
3. Are people with less money envious of rich people
4. Is money evil
5. Is health more valuable than money
6. How much money is a lot
7. Is time money
8. Does money make men more attractive
9. Does everyone want to be rich
10. Does money make more people who do not have a lot of it feel insecure
11. Do women secretly have an issue with a lover that earns less than they do
12. Do poorer people try to use richer people

13. Can money make people happy
14. Does a flawless diamond ring show more love than a copper ring
15. How can money hurt a relationship
16. Should poor people focus on getting money
17. What is money
18. Is a dead rich man richer than a live poor man
19. Why is money not important
20. Should we give money to beggars on the street
21. Does our society cater to money
22. Should we borrow money to buy things
23. Do poor people live happier lives outside the US
24. What is the best investment of money
25. Does money change a person
26. What is the worst way to spend money
27. How does not having money change a person
28. Should children be given money
29. Should couples focus their relationship on getting rich

30. Should churches ask for money

31. Why do some women talk down to men with money

32. Does a person really own a house if they are still paying for it

33. What does free mean

Are you tied up today

Friendship

1. Should people in a relationship disclose who all their friends are
2. Should people have sex with friends
3. What should we never do with a friend
4. What is a friend
5. Should you be friends with your ex
6. How many friends should people have
7. Do friendships have rules
8. Who should be allowed to choose our friends
9. What if the rules of the friendship are broken
10. Should married people have single friends
11. Is forgiveness a part of friendship
12. Is friendship a need or a want
13. Do friendships have limits
14. What should we expect from friends

15. What is a best friend
16. What should we give friends
17. what should we never say to friends
18. Should friends control friends
19. Should friends be reliable
20. Should we be friends with people who do not like each other
21. Are friends more likely to hurt a person than an obvious enemy
22. Is a dog man's best friend
23. Should friendship come before love in all cases
24. Is a diamond a girl's best friend
25. Can we trust most friends
26. What should we never tell a friend
27. When does friendship begin
28. Is there an age limit to being friends
29. When does friendship end
30. Should we expect birthday cards from friends
31. Should mom or dad always be a friend
32. Should friends have the same values

33. Should a teacher be friends with students

34. Why do girls say they make better friends with boys

35. Should high school students be friends with people older than 25 years of age

36. Should rich people with poor friends invite them to their home

37. What do friends owe us

Family

1. What is a family
2. What should not be part of a family
3. When is a family too big
4. Is stress part of a family
5. When should people start a family
6. What kind of people should not have a family
7. What is a good family
8. Who is the head of a family
9. Is there a loser in every family
10. Should all family members have the same values
11. Is a family by blood stronger than a family not tied by blood
12. Are rich families better off than poor families
13. Should we want to make our family bond

14. Should families dictate who a person should marry
15. When should family blessings be sought before marriage
16. Should families eat meals together
17. Should families move if the kids do not want to
18. How important is family honor
19. Do families have rules
20. What happens if family rules are broken
21. Who makes family rules
22. Should you turn your back on family
23. What do family members owe each other
24. Should teenagers be able to divorce parents legally
25. Should two parents work when they have an infant
26. Should in-laws be considered a part of the family
27. When should opinions of family members not count
28. Should family members loan money to each other
29. What things should husband and wife never tell other family members
30. Does being a family require blood or marriage

31. Should children be expected to go into the family business

32. Should families get counseling

33. Should families all go to the same church together

34. What should a person expect from family

35. What should we never take from family

36. Should everyone have a family

37. When should a person leave the family home

38. Whose family should be responsible for the cost of the wedding

39. Should family take sides in an argument

40. Should family members lie to each other

41. After parents divorce, what should you tell children about family

42. What does it mean to be considered family

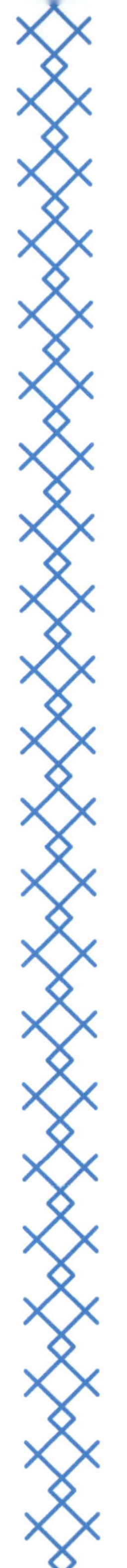

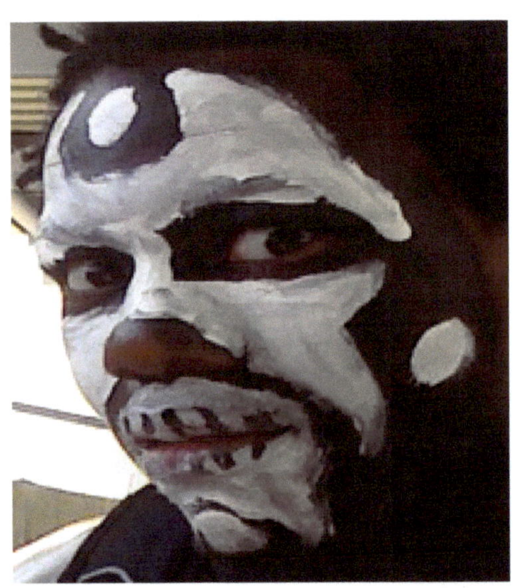

Boo!

Fear

1. What is fear
2. Where does fear come from
3. When are we in fear
4. Why do we fear
5. What do we fear
6. Do we need fear
7. Can we use fear
8. How can we use fear
9. Is fear good
10. Is fear bad
11. Do people fear falling in love
12. Should children fear parents
13. Is fear a part of faith
14. Is fear a part of religion

15. Is fear a part of politics

16. Is fear a part of love

17. Can we hide fear

18. Why do we hide fear

19. Does everyone have fear

20. Do we fear rejection

21. Do we fear death

22. Do we fear truth

23. Do we fear telling the truth or hearing it more

24. Do we fear police (government)

25. Do we fear being poor

26. Do we fear being alone

27. Do we fear doctors

28. Do we fear the unknown

29. Is fear rational

30. Can we manipulate fear

31. When should we use fear

32. Is fear related to needs

33. What do old people fear

34. What do teenagers fear

35. What do mothers fear

36. What do fathers fear

37. Is fear instinctual or learned

38. Do we fear failure

39. Do we fear getting old

40. How are truth and fear associated

Also by Peter John,

Hi, Have a Nice Day (H.A.N.D.)

Universal Music Group-OkTopUs Records

About the Author

Peter John, JD., MBA. Accomplished artist, author, talk-show host and world traveler Founder of Talk C.A.L.M (Communication And Learning Through Mediation). Billboard top 10 Artist.

Hobbies include theatre, flying airplanes, songwriting and traveling.
www.talkcalm.com

www.ingramcontent.com/pod-product-compliance
Lightning Source LLC
Chambersburg PA
CBHW040130270326
41928CB00001B/18
* 9 7 8 1 5 7 2 5 8 6 5 3 6 *